M000273156

Throwing Shadows

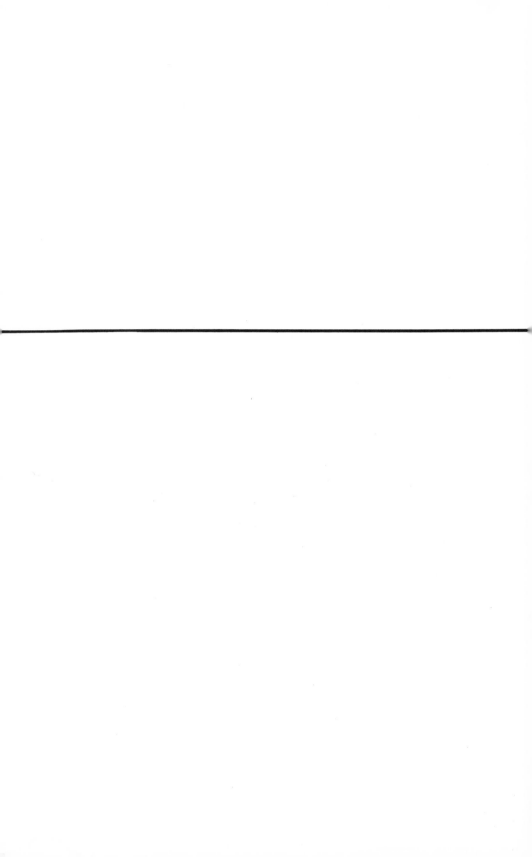

Throwing Shadows

POEMS BY KEN GERNER

 Copper Canyon Press · Port Townsend · 1985

Thanks to William O'Daly, editor at *Willow Springs* where several of the poems first appeared. "House of Breath" was first published as a pamphlet by Copper Canyon Press. "Glorious Without Knowing" was first published as a broadside by Jawbone Press.

Publication of this book was made possible in part by a grant from the National Endowment for the Arts.

ISBN 0-914742-87-6
LC # 84-73337

Copper Canyon Press   Box 271   Port Townsend, Wa 98368

For the land and family that raised me
and for Mara

CONTENTS

I.

Sitka Run

— for my father

I.
Something raises this old body,
heavy with smoke, distilled spirits,
the weight of the moon and displaced
hopes, from bed and weary
I stammer down to the shore

with thoughts of teaching children.
How to tell them what is in store,
the loves and hates they'll know and
too quickly, too slowly pass through,
that their parents didn't really mean
their lives and what they take for granted,
the flanks of woods and rush of clear water,
will pass. How to tell them their lives
will be cut or muddy with time, unless
there is the image. How that is all
and even that, at times, is not enough.

On rocks, fifty feet out
from the sea's edge, two immature bald eagles
preen and wait.
I recall the nights I spent
on the forks of the Flathead
waiting to spot them at dawn
trailing the kokanee run.
How rare and now
they are so simply here.

I sink and gain strength from the cold
reassurance of stone, watch my breath

join the fog, the open thermos
steams as the turn of tide chatters
and crows leave their caws
in flight
begin to articulate
delicate tongue calls on the wing
guttural
breath turns.

The green hump of Verstovia rises
behind me in the fog. Its false peak
erect behind, Arrowhead, still
holds winter tight to its crevasses.
Out in the sound, small islands green
real estate, now or soon, the preserve
of lawyers, doctors, this time's elite.
The cedar siding on their houses
begins to turn and bleach from wind
and rain like the clapboards that rattle
on the frames of deserted gold camps.

Beyond, the south shore swells the way
it always has, the steep slopes
hold the struggle of spruce, hemlock,
berry vine, snow water and stone.
There, bear learn to negotiate,
deer trail and eagles mate and anchor
nests they add to year after year.
A few crows and, occasionally, a raven.

II.
On a clear evening, I caught a boat ride
up Silver Bay, inland to the west, along
the north shore, past the smoking Japanese
mill that, for a few jobs, turns rafts

4

of timber into pulp, sends it all home
to make rayon that comes back to tourist
shops, orange T-shirts stenciled:
"Where the Hell is Sitka, Alaska?"

On past transplanted goats trapped in white
on cliffs and rocks in the fog,
past the dam at the bay's end with tunnels
blasted up to a lake whose water rushes
back down to the turbines that turn
to light the town and then we turned back

down the south shore, past the mouth
of the Salmon River where the chum
would be next to spawn, past log rafts
sporadically anchored safe from the wind.
There are no roads. That shore rises
without man back into itself and there,
for more than a moment, the ancient urge
told me to run, to confess I am not man.
I am better suited for duff,
for stalking with the bear,
rooting,
disappearing rather

than appearing here in Sitka,
though the footsteps I follow are honored.
Root, Cady, Hamill, Hedin taught here
and before them,
before the Russians cleared the glade
that is now the town stroll
called Totem Park after its poles,
imported art slashed from Prince of Wales
Island, before the Russians breached
the Tlingit fort that is now the clearing
crows silently ponder,

before them,
all those who taught
children still with wide eyes learning.

Last night, coming from the Columbia Bar,
past the marina
with boats kachunking the early dawn,
past crows beginning their hop
across telephone lines and down ramps,
I filled myself with ripening salmon berries,
thought of what I would tell the children
this last day
and saw the fur curling out my open collar
and crawling down my forearm.

III.
Tonight, I will lumber onto some jet
and watch the darkness crawl
from the east, over the innumerable shores
one must cross to get back south.
I will hope for a clear night
and moon when I get home,
to help tell him
what I have seen
like a shadow play
across the stars
and grow black and wish
to blend with the night.

Then the morning, hoping
I will leave with his call,
spring from his branch,
become breath on wing again.

Here, too, crow. Bodhidharma.

There, on Baranof Island, a sow bear
licks her berry-stained tongue
across her cub's snout,
sits back on her haunches
and waits.

High tide holds the Salmon River
to its banks and
something in the sound begins
its final run for home.

The Arousing

Back in the shallow wake laced with foam,
her mane takes the mighty arc of mare, dives
into the flare of breath, the claps of
cantering hooves turn into wind.

The cleft hills rumble, another is born
through the musk and whistles. From
the berry fat of sleeping bear, she
awakens, chest deep, her gasps claw the air

like desperate clouds, she plunges through
the snow, white as the fur that cloaks
her shank, taut on the faint edge of stone,
in the night, all the light there is beads

in her eyes. Her lips curl, spread the white
fire of teeth, with a cry, she dives down
through the open sky. She is the only thing
moving, cleaving the blue. She breaks in,

belly full of the fire of breath, she curls,
the sea boils over her back, the sounding.
Rising in the morning grass, a mouse, gray
as mist, dances with a dew-heavy stalk

for seed, her black eyes chip away at the sun
that shadows the fine roots. The flare
of knuckles emerges from the still air, her
fingers enchase a flowering mudra, one hand

changing into the other.
She is awakening.

The Sound's Edge

Scrub pine finger through
morning fog rising off
the sound. Weak sun finds
beads of mist dangling
the spider's web. You walk

the sandy shore. Drift
stacks a strange skeleton.
Its empty belly holds the dark
cry of wave. Your eyes
find amidst rubble of shells,

rocks, wood scraps, the laughter
of things as they might be.
The knuckle of bone turning
into a stone fist, the dance
of water and light breaking

sand into small stars, wood
flecks smoothed to flesh. This
is imagination and the sun
takes you to the top of bluffs
where things are as they are,

where trees have leaves and old
wood takes the silky dive into
earth, and thorns are still sharp.
Here you leave your eyes, once
again trust your fingers'

touch, follow the taut line
of horizon's curve all the way

to the opening, you lean slowly,
slowly turn to the lapping,
the lapping of the sea below.

Often at Night

I step to some vantage of sky.
This July, like some worn deity,
the new moon curls its ceremony
to Venus. On the horizon, sea clouds
break the lock of valley air, arch
their shell inland. Breeze oracles
rain to shivering leaves, like fear,
it crawls the nape of my neck.
In the small ravine,

              to the north,
grown thick with alder, vines and fir,
something scuttles in the brush.
Speculation would be satisfied to
identify it, but this body doesn't
know. Each night, there is the sound
I don't know. Each night, I am
pleased by it. While ears live
in the brush,

              eyes hold to the sky.
My breath recalls the edifice of
language strung between the two,
centuries of song rising from the earth,
within it the arrogance of proclamation
sinks, centuries of tongues lashing die.
What remains is the sound, circling
man and woman and child, celebrating
the kill,

        the one who got away,
some goddess or god,

coyote or spider.
The song remains,
not lover or loved,
but their breathing
laughter
crying
      now that rustle in the brush
and the moon's claw against the night.

Dithyramb

The stars and the rivers
and waves call you back.
— Pindar

Day begins with night, night with prayer.
Father, keep my soul. Mother, bless me.
Mother, bless me. Father, keep my soul
safe in its wanderings through night. Mother,
rock this body I lay down, this body I give back.

In darkness, we begin. We speak the same
language, understand there is no understanding.
It's night. Darkness doesn't mean this.
There is no face behind the mask. There
is no mask. That is day and day begins

with night. The gape of chaos shudders
the egg open. The concussion of black
wings thunders open the night, cracks
the void into shell. Sky here, Ouranos.
Earth there, Gaia. In the night, we
all speak the same language and
Eros is born. Mother, rock this

body. How do we move in the dark? Eros
taught us, before he was weighed down
with wings and arrows, before daylight made him
a cruel boy. Eros knows, move where you like,
love is attraction, the force that pulls the hand,
the wing, the paw. It is the same language
in the night. We all know it. Father,

keep my soul. Sky there, Ouranos. Earth
here, Gaia. Eros between. He is one
son. There are more, waiting in the night.
Day begins with night, with the slice of black
wings, the curl of paw, the cut of sword.
There are no masks in the dark, no face
behind the mask. Mother, rock this body

I give back. The gape of chaos, the wound is
open. This is attraction. Not the prick of
an arrow or a snicker in the bushes. There
are no masks, only blood runs in the night.
Father, Mother, Son, now Daughter. The same
turning. In the darkness, this makes sense.
It has to. Day begins with night and we speak alike.

Black blood etches the foam of the sea. Black
winged bird thunders the universe and from
the shell of blood and foam, Aphrodite is born
from the sea, the black sea, the night and
blood. Mother, rock this body I lay down.

Father, the Sky, Ouranos.
Mother, the Earth, Gaia.
Son, always between, Eros.
Night cuts this trinity. Darkness,
the gape through which the Daughter,
Aphrodite, rises bloody from the sea,
the gape through which daylight moves.

Day begins with night,
where my soul is safe
in its wanderings. Night begins
with prayer, where we all speak
the same language.

II.

The Moon Year

after Li Ho (791-817)
for Kenneth Rexroth (1905-1982)

First Moon

Cross the bed of pine needles,
swing the gate open to spring's coming.
The night is crouched into itself,
the white sun held in its claw.
Bow into this silence, bow to
the demons of winter's barren dreams,
bow to the passing.

A long bubble sucks flat
to the milky tatter of ice
that clings to the stream's bank.
The air sack pulses with the current,
wriggles free, disappears.
The broken pearl of winter's last moon
has set. In the dark, draw
the first cold drink of spring.

Sunlight will come, wake the croci,
open knots of bud to holiday and
seduce the delicate flower of luck.
In its shadow, the tiger
of night will gamble.

Asleep in a cocoon of red silk,
she curls from the cold into herself.
The shadows to flag this dawn
are yet to grow across her cheek,
across her ivory mask of sleep.

Second Moon

I drink last year's wine by the stream
where mint now greens and cherry
blossoms ready to burst their sheaths.

Yellow blossoms of sallow await
hungry tongues of butterflies.
Mountains turn to jade.
All the growing plants resound.
The dog's bark sets the tree tops swaying.
Huge manes shake free from spring rain.

White silk clings to the hollow of her
hips, shadows her spin across the floor
of sky. The wind, a bamboo flute,
accompanies. The deep rumble of
a dragon-coiled thundercloud strums
the taut silk-spun string
of her body. Bright
streamers snap out around her.
A thousand arms surround her dance.

Evening comes early, still echoes
the stone cold chime of winter.
The green frog won't sing tonight.
Only the small comfort of this wine
is left. While in anxious sleep,
young women coax fox, badger,
weasel from their winter burrows.

Third Moon

East wind harps the pines.
Yellow pollen frosts the crystal air,
dusts the shoulders of farmers
bent to open the ground.
Swallows salvage mud
to house their return.

The rising sun licks through
the jostle of willow, a tongue
of fire on the stream bank.
New green waves on the graves
of the dead, with the living,
willing slaves to buds, shoots,
roots that weave the earth.

My eyelids grow heavy
with the petals of spring.
White sheets of writing paper
pray to be filled.

The wind scatters
the thousand blossoms, rivers
their scent to the west.
It is this she trusts to take her
sweet perfume, while
for the evening alone,
she shadows her eyes.

Fourth Moon

Leaves grow into their green,
what blossoms are left curl
to crescents in their shade.
Swallows chatter in the beams.

Peonies have found the will
to open, the high sun spins
their colors: water that sleeps
in moonlight, black robe stained
with wine. A stunted seed pod,
twisted loose by the breeze,
drops into the blue pond.
The ripples don't last long.
The golden carp don't blink.

The warmth and dazzle of summer
depress me, no money to pilgrimage,
to return to memories, to leave
the city's walls. The rich caravan
to mountain shrines.

In the park, mothers, grandmothers,
doting girls play with their young.
In the cool shade of the trees,
who is that man shredding petals,
singing and beating time,
alone with his bottle of wine?

Fifth Moon

The river's current slices and twists
the cloud of moon into a host of lanterns.
Thermal winds sigh through pines.
Lament the drowned ones. The sun is down.
A resident pair of ducks fly the dark shore,
the flutter of wings cut into the night.

You held that rock like an amulet close
to your heart, like it was the last
piece of luck in the world.
You had tired of enticing her
with wild golden flights across
the sky, tired of your tricks
played out on high winds.
So you came back to earth
where you could name flowers
and took to throwing them
across the dark longing of her eyes.

Magnolias, orchids, melilotus,
petals strewn to hold her,
glistened like jewels of sweat
on her body, eddied and pooled
and ran down her dancing,
escaped from the swaying dark
tresses of her hair.
They soon lost their perfume,
not even time could bring them back.
You had thought at least
you could count on flowers.

What else could break through,
what was left, but the stone and you
the only one to build her a home
within the water. It was something
to hold, to weight you from the sky.
Unlike the delicate petals that
flew from your grasp, that stone
was firm to your embrace.

As you felt its cool press
against your breast, it was like her,
like the mornings you'd seen her shadow
twist and splay in the mist, the mornings
you took the dew as her caress.
As its weight pulled river into lake,
you felt your joy slowly sink
into the jade pool of her eyes.

The bubbles of your breath rose
like pearls through the dark clutch
of water. As you sank, wave after wave
came down to welcome you, Ch'ü Yüan,
and you held to the stone,
your final gift to her.

The nights will now grow longer.
I see her flower in the moonlight,
hear her laughter ripple the night,
daring me to fly.

Sixth Moon

The earth is sore with the red sun.
Willow branches sweep the yellow grass.
Leaves turn their silver charms
to face the dry wind. A turtle
stares from leather leaves
stretching across the lotus pond.

Caught in her dressing mirror,
the sun's mirror of flame finds her,
dissolves into lightning, turns
to black and green coils around her.
Thunder beats a continuous roll
across the drum of sky.

Shadows of freshly washed hair
spoke across her bowed shoulders,
a wheel of white petals jeweled
with the pleasures of rain.

Seventh Moon

Starlight grows ripe
in the lengthening night, the cricket's
song whirrs in the rocks.
Bells clang, as cows come down
from summer grazing grounds.

Dripping from the stream's bath,
she rises to the wind's chill.
Clad only in the raiment of flesh,
she steps onto the bridge of wings,
the black, lonely shore of night.

There, she awaits his warmth,
smells the musk, feels the steam
of his body encircle her. The only
cloth she cannot weave herself.

Wrapped in this cloak,
her hands fall idle
in their days of languor.
The sky grows cold,
naked to her eyes.
Tears and rain
raise a silver river

between them.
Invisible processions of the dead
throng the night sky.
Candles float out on the river.
A field of flame.
Bonfire for what is past.

Eighth Moon

Things have grown round.
They hunger to be held
by earth. Ripe
on the roadside, fat
black molecules of berries
suck from stems.
Apples, streaked red,
tug free from bent boughs,
thunk with the sound
of their juice. Melons
sink in the ground, holding
pools of sweetness inside
thick skins. Globes
of peaches, all turning
round and down. Perfectly
round, the autumn moon holds
herself high in the heavens.

Her arms of light move
across the scales of night,
comfort all things
with their measure.
Moon smooths the wrinkles
from my weary face,
turns to cool wine,
the air I breathe.
Her light lends grace
to the silhouette
of my awkward wanderings.

The many nights
these tired eyes

have held her.
The many times
this hand has
poised to write
I am coming home.

Ninth Moon

Slow with the tailings of summer,
the narrow stream whispers
like the rustle of raw silk.
Drying alder leaves chatter
in the breeze. The cricket's song
shadows me wherever I move.

In daylight, I climbed the heights,
left the rumble of the city,
the weight of moths and slow flies.
I rose above timberline,
over talus slopes, pulled up
through a rock chimney until
there was nothing left except
myself and the shrine of sky.

The wheel of the hawk rose
between us. The strong wind
made a song of the dry stalks
of bear grass. The kite of my body
filled with the world's breath.
Soon, there will be only snow.

Now, by the stream, the cold
dew crawls up my pantlegs.
Night takes the last croak
from the crow and the colors
from my eyes. From the cave
of underbrush, a night creature
cracks awake.

With wine, I try to sweep
clean the graves inside.
Drink sinks like sap into the dark,
leaves what is above ground
to the turning fall.

Tenth Moon

Mountain peaks are buried
in the belly of cloud.
Fingers of fog trace
the furrow of each watershed.
The rendezvous that held
my hopes is frozen fast.
Wind has spun the colored leaves
to weave with the earth.
Frost burns the ribbon
of stream, kingfisher blue.

Stars spill
from the crystal cup
of moon. In the cold dark
before dawn, snowflakes drift
down the valley's clear sky.

Silence grips the shadows
like ice. Breath
clings white to my beard.

Eleventh Moon

Cold wind pierces the bare trellis of alder.
Frost laces the empty bench that
held the embrace of warmer nights.
Creatures slow in their fur coats.
Bears hole up in sleep.
Waterfalls hang in silence.
I dream of migrant geese.

It has been days since light
broke the thick cover of cloud.
Circling on their dim course,
the sun, the moon, seem erratic.
Darkness stretches ten thousand miles.
Chill cuts through my clothes,
stills my heart as I await
the thaw of dawn.

Only yesterday, I pleaded
for the night to hold the moonlight
closer to our touch. Now,
this longest night, she is far away,
beyond clouds, her bangles of white jade
slowly swinging, her echo
clinking through halls of ice.

Twelfth Moon

Before dawn, weak light breaks
red through windows
of houses clustered in
the hollow. Morning,
the many lives scatter

from the common bed of sleep.
Cold stars recede
through bare branches
of fruit trees, the fruits of summer
are gone, gone.
The moon remains.

The long nights end.
The long days begin.

Intercalary Month

We are certain of the time of coronation,
seldom death. Sunlight is accurately
recorded. The calendar is stuffed.

The blood let in its time, the smile
of the weasel, knows no end, only
accurate parts. These days are
numbered, the turning of blossom
to fruit, the circle of shadows
longing, the spin of repetition,
the remorseless accuracy of change.

Now darkness turns in upon itself.
Moonlight is cut by a measure
not its own, its shadow thrown
away to void, where it is possible to
dream of laughing, where any voice can
speak and the hand of caress is chosen.

The picking of peaches, our labor, is
for the day and timely.

The drinking of that wine, our love, is
for night and seamless.

III.

Tracking

As a kid
I tracked down
wounded ducks
along the riverbottom.

Webbed feet and
pink blood sinking
in the snow,

they would head
for the brush,
thick tangles
of young willows,
winter naked and yellow,

hide in beds of old
leaves, alone with fear
climbing out their eyes.

As they died
in my hands,
I thought of warm marshes
and bays to the south,
how hard it is
to get there.

Once in Passing

—for Sam Hamill

To the west, the Bitterroot Range rises,
Chief Joseph, St. Mary's, Sky Pilot.
Canyons drop deep and true, Bass Creek,
Big Creek, Sweathouse. Peaks split
the timberline. Wind and snow stunted
pine turn to talus slopes and nothing else
but snow, unless it's summer and there's
phlox, huckleberry brush, bear grass,
the blood red blossoms of paintbrush on
the edge of a ridge. Farther back,
the wilderness holds to itself, Diablo
Mountain, hanging lakes, moose bogs,
cliff swallows and hoodoos in the fog.

Along the east, the Sapphires roll, smooth
hills with no distinction for memory to claim.
Long, languid cuts lay the streams through
wheat fields to the valley floor. Burnt Fork,
Three Mile. Spring rains on dry slopes
coax petals of bitterroots from sandy soil.
North of here, Charlo's smile clinked
like gambling bones. He taught American
history with the story of Robber's Rules,
how majority rules. How the least are voted
to be sacrifice. The last white buffalo
died in the north. Bitter roots white
amidst the dusty turquoise of sagebrush.

Between these lies the valley. It's evening.
I'm a young one. The wind moves down river,
cools the sweat on my bare chest caked with

the chaff of haying. Hot muscles tighten
as they come to rest. I walk to the shade
of the shop to taste the metal of a cold beer
and watch sparks fly from sickles
being sharpened for tomorrow's mowing.

Across the river, a young woman sings
to the slow trek of Holsteins
to the milking shed. Their heavy udders
swish between their legs. She walks
behind with a willow switch, cooing
"Come, cow. Come, cow," to their going.
Later, my nostrils fill with the thick
sweetness of the iodine she uses to clean
the milk lines and buckets. In what is
left of the day's light, I touch
the whiteness of her skin. In the dusk,
we splash and laugh, swim in the slough
still warm with the Bitterroot sun.

Like you, I could tell how it all changed.
It's never a mystery, what day the subdivider
moves in, what day the banker builds his ranch-
house on the hill that was an alfalfa field,
how the clear-cuts rise to the horizon,
how the sick green of sewer moss fills the streams,
how the retirees die with their money and
what is around them, how corporations conspire
to raise hay and wheat and cattle at a loss,
how they never go broke, how the price of gas
breaks farmers, how coal mines and cities
steal their children and how business is happy.

I could tell how I don't know where everyone
went, how I know they're gone, how elk herds
and deer became the reserve of the airborne

Californians, how I've watched the shadow
of the western peaks close across the valley
to night. But the telling doesn't change
the present and one can only witness so long,
before the testimony sounds false.

You have the desert crying beneath
the flood of memory. Some days,
brother, I see you move slow, as though
underwater, like the fleshy skeleton
of an old cottonwood bowing to the weight
of water as it sinks in the sludge that
fills the bottom of some dammed canyon.
In your eyes, I've seen light undulate
like sunlight on the slickrock outside
your Moab home, how you wrestle through
the days sure as a sidewinder. Now,
moved to the edge, you live by the sea,
the water of the sound. You embrace
the beast, the brine screams in it,
salt from the land that raised you.
It's always there. To your house
nestled in second growth over
the peninsula's end, you still haul
water from town. Waterbags to the desert,
friend, even there, at home,
there's not enough pure water.
It's gone.

And I sit evenings away in the dark
corner of some beaten tavern, where
plastic mounts of deer and bear hang
to advertise with their death some sweet
liquid of forgetfulness and at times
when I'm not overcome with the simple
reverberation of the body's temple bells,

I think back to the high hollows that
elk are driven to, to the red blotch
in the snow, where a cow aborts
for lack of the valley's browse, her
ribs shudder around the deepest breath,
the involuntary strain of flanks, that
look of question living in her eyes,
larger than pain, how then another step
is taken, the beginning of another path
broken in the snow, and I think of how
I'm not there, how I save her a moment
of shock at my sight. Because I sit
here, one elk has a few more heartbeats,
the earth a few less scars. By absence,
I add to the stillness of the wilderness.
How little my life is to that, how little
the sacrifice and yet in this present,
brother, in our songs of love, we learn.

One knows one is nothing, that what one
knows is nothing, that only the pain
of the passing convinces us it is real,
once, and once only, and teaches us
care. We are left in the cold air
of solitude from which we embrace and
sing through the pain to each other,
man to man, each father, brother, son.
How we leave our scars and gossip
like women, "Do you know what happened,
have you heard?"

Now as time chinks your face, as
the expansion of ice splits the desert
stone, you turn occasionally to the sea
as though it were a woman and try
to make of this present, a past

of labor and love. I know the struggle,
the ghosts that tear one from the task.
You sit in that spot, private as blood,
on the edge of the sound, a widow with
eyes on the sea, full with the question
that has no answer. It comes before.
It is answer like Eden is answer, like
the landscape of our growing is answer,
like grass prairies stripped for coal,
like flooded desert canyon floors, earth
under asphalt, mornings after the death
of love when perfume hangs sweet
in the air, like a red fetus frozen
in the snow, hope turned to a blotch
of blood and naked and cold and lone,
we raise the weary foot, the question,
for one more step into the cold, one more
step to print the trail that may come
to haunt us with its love.

Right action is all that is ever left,
to cleave to the common, to split wood,
care for the children, cultivate gentleness,
caress the freedom of all we know, to sit
by the hole our breath keeps free of ice,
the hole we call present, wait there without
spear or line, only an open heart and hand,
wait through the eternity to hear the return
of another's breath, its glistening hide,
its cool suck, the shimmer of bear grass in
the rain, the slow heave of the desert hills
as they turn the twilight red.

Shadows

*"Between Chuang Chou and
a butterfly there must be
some distinction."*
— Chuang Tzu

I.
Through the day, he walks
as though he knew the way.
His hands carry a flower,
a book, an axe, or nothing.
He usually has a shadow
depending on the light.

II.
Leaves in summer lace
the ground with shadow.
In winter, the leaves
are gone. Their shadows
are gone too.

III.
There is a child in a room.
There is a candle and her
hand throws shadows on
the wall: rabbits, coyotes,
disfigured old women. We hear
her laughter cut through the night.

IV.
In the pool, the trout
loll, face upstream, below
on the moss and gravel
their shadows lie, twitching
and disconnected. We think
it is a matter of suspension,
not fear, that our shadows
are always attached to us.

V.
A match is struck.
Everything we see
in the room has
a shadow.

VI.
A rock doesn't
move. Its shadow
moves all around,
back and forth.

VII.
When the hawk dives
straight down, its shadow
races across the field
to catch up with it.
This makes sense to us.

VIII.
In the moonless night,
he tells her of these things.
As they turn to sleep, back

to back, a black butterfly
opens its invisible wings,
beats them once, then it is
two. Butterflies fill the room.
In the dark, in the silence,
we can hear the breathing
shadows of butterflies.

For a Friend

— for Stefanie

Words pulled into the long silence
of night, fill each morning. Screams
of the dreamer cringe in each lengthening
shadow. Night's celebrants pace
the streets, listen for what it was
they said. The unfortunate wonder why.
The "iloveyous" turn to limp hands that
stroke the empty daylight.

                  What words
that might stick, that could breach
the daylight whole with their origin are
covered in an avalanche of "goodmornings,
howareyous, nice days." They forget
themselves. This night, resolve to speak
to nothing you cannot

                  touch, turn your back
on the moon. Make love to whom you love
without a word. When they turn to sleep
and the darkness deepens, don't listen to
their dreams or your own. When tears
come, taste their salt

                and know that.
The silence, let that hold you now and don't
say a thing, let morning come, feel
the stars still on your back, know that it
is always night.

Do this for days and nights,
until there is no difference, until your tongue
has lost its reflex and your mind wakens
to only what your hands, your eyes, perceive.
Do this until your mind is no more your mind.

Then some word will rise, you will hear
your breathing say *friend*, you will find
your tongue touch the roof of your mouth
at the word's end, feel how complete it is.
Friend, you will say and hear the birds

for the first time — it will be your lover's
fingers through your hair. *Friend*, you
will hear it for the first time and the moon
will laugh with you and it won't be day

or night, and you won't be you and the word
will stick and I don't know if it's true, but
I had to write this so we could know
what it is when we become each other's
eyes and our tongue takes an old path

and we hear the word, *friend*,
and don't know who said it.

Poem

The year's yellow petals fall
from a peace rose in Kalispell.
Honkers push the sun south.
Letters yellow to the center.

Words, walls, snowbound in Missoula,
the stones kept in a sack,
the stray white cat
where they began to change,

I began to have a past.
This isn't the first leaf
I've seen brown and drop.
Could I have know that before

or where you sleep,
the hours of your dreams,
the fraying of the upholstery
the bed sagging to the middle,

or what it means to be weaned
in the fall, before the snow?

Countenance

Cold rain falls, silver in the slant of evening
sunlight. Crows preen, right their flight
feathers for the night. High fir boughs
shadow the wind's return. The door closes.
Silence becomes ours. Conversation trails
on by itself, keeping its own distance.
One hand on the water tap starts a flow

that begins miles from here. The chair
cracks, the cross of stockinged legs, the clack
of a shoe, a floor joist groans, a calendar page
waves in the rising heat. Potatoes peeled white
lie next to the steel sink. The cold and coming

night make the house a skin we wear. In it, we
tell of happenings across the hill, cut meat, and
warm ourselves with tea. In the dark, I've tried
to match my breath to yours, moved my arm
in and across the cold to question your shoulder
into turning, then listened as your breath
became echo,

        heard the ticking of the heater
contracting, the fir limbs scrape across shingles,
watched the clouds swell across the moon, saw
the black veins of night root through the sky to
become sheaths through which nothing passed, but
the drone of earth as it spun itself another day.

The dishwater warms my hands. The thrash
of crows, now still. My thoughts follow the water
back into night, back to its deep black pool

at the foot of the old volcano and its wealth of
snow, then back again to its dance as it showers
you, silver with the reflection of light enclosed
in that room, enclosed in the house.

                                    As I step
into the dark, my wet hands chill, my breath
clouds, steam curls from your bowed
back and black hair, and nothing makes a sound.

IV.

Memory

In the turning fall,
you walk the leaf-
mottled paths, the earth
stranded in the fog,
in the breath of all
the stones.

You stoop to the stream's
edge, cup the cold
water, stilling the rush
in your hands. Your lips
shape the smile you wear
for her.

Around you, aging alder
splay for the sun,
from the duff, the stones
hump, gentled by the glove
of moss. Here and there,
a bare crystal shard

seizes a lank of sunlight,
twists it to fire.

House of Breath

Over the Coast Range, silver horns of cloud
darken to rose. The fire is set. The crackle
and pop of pitch and kindling burn into logs.
I split ribs for dinner, aware of thin muscles
that hold the dark cave of breath. This house

welcomes as winter approaches. There were others.
One of logs in a valley in the Rockies, where
I was raised rough-housing with my father
and brothers. The years winter ran late,
my father's hands cracked from the waters
of calving and wind. Later, that wind
out of the Gulf of Alaska bowed the tops

of second-growth on the peninsula's tip. Inside,
warm, I watched chunks of turnips and spuds
fall into the pot of stew as I talked with
friends in their house of poetry and printing,
of what it is to love something, anything.
Bourbon has never been so smooth. Searing ribs.

Soon my love will return to enter this warmth,
the cascade of smells and she will smile at the half-
empty bottle. I will sit as this house asks her
what she remembers, watch as her children dance
across her eyes. The warmth of other fires
will become her arms curled under her breasts,
around the rise and fall of her breathing.

And then one of us will say something silly,
like 'how's your ass' and laugh at the infinity
of intention and the simple charms we use

to enter the silence. Outside, the wind
will come with its dreams of snow. We will
be shadows crossing shafts of yellow light.

Fat from the ribs will shine our cheeks as
we eat by the fire and coals will glow
as we make love beside bowls of bones and
light echoing in glasses empty of wine.

In the morning, I will leave the warmth of bed.
There will be frost and the cold floor.
The rags of alder leaves droop as I step outside
to sit with the morning, to watch smoke drift
from houses in this hollow. Cold and empty,
my lungs will fill and my ribs shudder around
and hold to the fine precision of breath.

Sister Dawn

In the alder, before dawn, the birds
rustle a prelude to morning flights.
Nuthatch, towhee, finch, old friends.
Upstairs, your breathing dreams.
You fly and grasses lick, dampen
your belly. The wolf with flames
for eyes and the tongue of moonlight
is with you. In your dressing mirror,

my writing light and the gray curve
of dawn meet. There each morning, you
kneel, hair pinned in the ancient manner,
your unveiled nape curves to the adornment,
your slender fingers track the gentle tuck
of eyelids and burnish the arc of cheeks
that already glow with the night.

The silken veil, that delicate membrane
that contains us. Skin. How women add to
and men continually take away. How nothing
is more naked than the face painted in celebration.
This morning, I steal to that cloud of mirror
while you sleep. Open my pouch of ash, mix it
with the tar of clay and dust of bone.

With this hand, the earth has given strength,
I stroke ashen lines across my face. In this
mirror, woman, we meet. The rough earth you fly,
the contour of my brow, the dew, tears. The flame
that is the wolf's eyes is this mirror and
the moonlight, this very dawn I turn to.

The house is quiet, filled with the heavy breath
of night, the nuthatch begins his scratch and
the towhee her rough song. The contractions
of the drying clay join my lips to the word,
brother. *Brother Night.* I hear in the syllabic
pulses of blood, the word, sister. *Sister Dawn.*

The morning light now jewels the bevels
of your dressing mirror. Whatever face I had
is gone. Only the laughter of a woman's eyes,
that flame so like a wolf and moonlight, remains.
You sit to your dressing mirror and gaze
beyond, outside to the alder, the finches,
my eyes, now the shadows of their flight.

Black Beginning

The nights circle his eyes,
cut them like lake shores,

the ebb and flow of hope,
crows, heavier tracks,

things that land only to fly.
He feels the rustle and hears

the scream of black form
the call that wakes him

to recount his memories like
loose change, to see what night took.

What is left, he hordes until
the morning; dawn breaks him.

Wild Geese Flying on Their Backs

My love has left for the north.
Now as fall clouds the Yukon,
the birch golden, the river slows.
Where she walks, the spruce darken.

Here, the maple has just begun
to turn red. The morning fog,
a little slower to part, holds
the bark of migrating geese.

They come from the north, echoing
vees, search for fallen seeds
in drying marshes and grain fields,
leaving the Arctic slope to ice.

The nights grow long with her
leave and gnaw. The humpback moon
hangs like a cracked eggshell,
an amber robe for an empty night.

In candlelight, her back once curved
like a shallow moonlit river, the way
the geese must feel the tundra split
and I felt the thrust of spring return —

the thrust that flies the geese back
to the edge, where the fire splits
their spine and the sun cracks
the white shell of ice and more

than the night flies out.

Name Is Only the Guest of Reality

— Hsü Yu

In the cold, breath
huddles to itself,
clouds with other clouds.
From the clouds of all
the breath, dew falls.

Our tongues knock
on the distance
all the stars hold.
Whose home is this?
Who's home?

As *dawn* edges
its shadow across
the meadow, it invites
grass. The tawny flank
draws in *elk*. *Tree*
comes out surrounding
and higher, *sky*
enters the vast blue.

In the space,
in the time,
that composes every thing
as a different thing,
there is a home,
where every name is
greeted, served,
then sent on its way.

There are times and places
where the names gather
and are at ease, together
they dance and sing
of a home where
what is called, answers

and, for a moment,
we feel welcome.

Glorious without Knowing

The rains come early. The drops nipple
the bottoms of ripening blackberries
and patter on broader alder leaves.
My right hand assures me the moon is waning.

Aging is no longer personal. Each day
I read, I touch the seal, the whale,
the cedar that is gone, the child, all
that is going. The gong of the dead sun
brings all hands to what home is.

I come with wine to sit with the wind
beneath the fir that are here and were
before my grandfather's thought. The jays
and the juncos watch me drink and the coming
night coaxes me to stay longer.

When the murmur of my love calls, the seed
of other men, other women, planted in
forests and hovels, hotels and fields,
the seed planted and replanted in the play
of light in time will come to this: her arms
will open all arms and with this gift,
the shores of night are not far off.

Her arms find me tonight in the dripping
of rain from fir and berries and with each
immersion, I ask the forgiveness of release.
I return to the world of promise that
filled the arms of our forebearers before

they touched what they thought was gold or
life. To say, *here it ends.* This night,
I stalk the silent fullness of what is
all ready in the opening, to give my love
that same distance in which she will rise

like the fir and ripen with the berries,
glorious without knowing, to share
the sweetness of the wind as it flaps
the alder, whooshes fir needles,
slants the rain and says, *I am going,*
but you, you are here, where you belong.